MW01127483

Positive Affirmations Journal

Susan LaBorde

Positive Affirmations Journal:
100 Journal Writing Prompts to Explore Your Thoughts, Focus on the Positive, and Visualize the Life You Really Want

Book Cover Design by Susan LaBorde

ISBN: 1532822871
ISBN-13: 978-1532822872

About Positive Affirmations

Far too often, the trouble with positive affirmations is that they aren't believable. You put on your happy face and your very best intentions, but try as you might, the words don't ring true. You know it because you feel the resistance in your gut.

This journal was created to help you remedy that by delving deeper and looking beyond mere words. To begin, one important aspect is awareness.

Most of us have a tremendous amount of negative self-talk going on in our heads all the time. We become so accustomed to it that we don't even recognize a negative thought when we have one. In fact, much of that negative thinking occurs just below our usual level of consciousness.

Journaling is an excellent way to explore your mind and identify the good, the not so helpful, and the downright destructive. After all, to get to where you want to be, you first need to understand where you are right now.

A second key aspect of this process is focus. What's interesting here is that this does not involve taking some specific action. It's not about what to do, but rather about what to stop doing.

In order to allow yourself to focus on the positive, you must first learn to let go of the negative. It's that simple. However, that doesn't mean it's always easy.

In some cases, letting go may require a lot of work, and journaling can be a very helpful tool. By taking the time to think and write, you stop allowing your brain to run on autopilot.

Only by letting go of the negative can we allow in the positive. With negative thinking we have limited options because we're blinded by tunnel vision. With positive thinking our options are limitless because our minds are open to all the endless possibilities.

A third crucial aspect of positive affirmations – last here but by no means least – is clarity.

It's been said that most of us don't get what we want out of life because we don't really know what we want. A perfect example of that is the desire for abundance.

Let's say that your morning affirmation is "I want more money." You head off to work, and as you're walking into your office building you find a penny on the sidewalk. Are you leaping with joy because you just manifested "more money"? My guess is, probably not.

Daily living has a way of keeping us too busy to give much thought to what matters most to us. All our time is devoted to checking off every item on that to-do list, and hurrying up about it so we can get a little sleep before we have to get up and make out tomorrow's list.

Over time our hopes and dreams can fade to little more than a vague desire for "something better". There is no clarity in that, and it certainly doesn't make for a very good affirmation.

Consider abundance again. Most everyone seems to want more money, but very few have any clear ideas about exactly what difference that would make in their lives and why it matters to them.

Do you want a new house? Really? Why? Compared to where you live now, would it be bigger? Smaller? In a different location? Would it have a grand formal dining room for elegant entertaining? Or a huge backyard pool where all your family can hang out every weekend? Or both?

The same applies to any desire you may have, from your material possessions to your personal relationships to your spiritual life. Nothing is likely to change for the better if you haven't defined what "better" means.

One of the best ways to improve on clarity is to put your thoughts in writing, and include lots of specific details. Most important, though, are your feelings. Perhaps you've already envisioned something specific that you want, down to the last lovely detail. That's a great start, but a key factor is the "why".

Especially when it comes to material possessions, it's never the thing itself that we want. It's how that thing will make life better for us in some way.

Whatever your desire, one crucial question to ask is, when you do receive this "thing", when what you want becomes a reality in your life, how will you feel?

Compare it to a meaningless daydream. I might momentarily entertain myself thinking of what it would be like to go skydiving. Part of me thinks it's fun to fantasize about the thrill of soaring through the air like a bird. Yet in reality, that is not something I actually want to do. Ever.

On the other hand, the desires that are truly important to us stir our passion, and that plays a vital role in our affirmations. No longer are we repeating meaningless words. Instead, we have a definite idea of exactly what we want, and we already feel an emotional connection to it.

At this point you are using the most powerful technique of all, and that is visualization. Don't be surprised when some of the prompts in this journal ask you to draw. If you can't draw or hate to draw, you can certainly write instead. The point is to encourage you to create a mental image in colorful, vivid detail. Make it so clear that you envision yourself already being, doing, or having what you declare in your affirmations – and so clear that you are already experiencing the emotions in the moment.

Now *that* is a powerful positive affirmation!

How to Use This Journal

As you write your way through this journal, keep in mind this one strict rule:

Rule #1 – There are NO rules!

Each of us is a gloriously unique human being, and so are our hopes, dreams, and aspirations. The affirmations in this journal cover a broad range of topics, which you are encouraged to interpret in any way you like.

If by chance you come across an affirmation or prompt that doesn't resonate with you, strike that one out and write your own! For example, some of the affirmations on family relationships could easily apply to a significant other instead. It's your journal, and it's your life, so please enjoy the freedom of making it exactly what serves you best.

You will notice that every affirmation is listed twice, and that is intentional. Each affirmation has two different prompts so that you have two ways to approach the topic, the purpose being to help you dig deeper. If you feel stuck on one or the other simply move on and come back to it later. As I said, there are no rules!

Most important is to get started. Explore what's going on inside your head, identify those unhelpful thoughts and begin the process of turning your focus from negative to positive. Discover what needs letting go in order to allow in the new. Visualize what you truly want to be, do, or have, and make the choice to change your attitude and improve your life.

Wishing you love, peace, joy, and abundance in every aspect of your life,

Susan

This journal belongs to

_____

I love myself and I allow myself to be loved fully.

Write a compassionate, loving, and non-judgmental description of yourself.

I love myself and I allow myself to be loved fully.

List 3 compliments you have received. Take a moment to think about each one, accept it completely, and write a heartfelt thank you.

In this moment I feel peaceful and content.

Picture yourself politely escorting your disturbing thoughts into an imaginary waiting room. How does it feel to have a temporary break from them?

In this moment I feel peaceful and content.

List everything, big and small, that you can feel peaceful about in this present moment.

I am enjoying the life I'm living.

What are your favorite simple pleasures, and why do you enjoy them?

I am enjoying the life I'm living.

Envision yourself having pleasant experiences every single day. What are you doing differently that is making life more enjoyable?

My thoughts are my reality, and I have the power to change my thoughts.

Observe your unwanted thoughts to see what you can learn. How can you use what you do not want to get clearer about what you do want?

My thoughts are my reality, and I have the power to change my thoughts.

Make your attitude adjustment list. When negative thoughts intrude, I can always choose to think about:

I release all resistance to feeling good.

I will feel better when ... what are you waiting on? Let it go by making a list using this statement: I am no longer waiting until _____ to feel better.

I release all resistance to feeling good.

Imagine every last feeling of resistance melting away, and list 3 things you can feel good about right this very moment.

Even the simple things in life bring me joy.

If you could see your average days through the eyes of a child, what insignificant moments would make you smile or laugh?

Even the simple things in life bring me joy.

Looking toward the week ahead, what opportunities will you have to look for joy in ordinary places?

Happiness is always available to me, and I choose to see it everywhere.

Draw a dark, gloomy day. Imagine yourself there, think of a reason to be happy, and write about it.

Happiness is always available to me, and I choose to see it everywhere.

Draw a beautiful sunny day. Create a mantra about always choosing happiness, and cultivate a habit of making this your first thought each morning.

I naturally attract loving relationships into my life.

Explain what you desire in a loving relationship, including your personal values and boundaries.

I naturally attract loving relationships into my life.

Thinking of an existing or future relationship, imagine that it is perfect and describe your experiences and emotions.

I accept and appreciate my body as a reflection of the unique being that I am.

Think of what is unusual about your shape or appearance, and list each thought in a kind, accepting way.

I accept and appreciate my body as a reflection of the unique being that I am.

Imagine being completely comfortable in your own skin, free of all urges to criticize your body. Describe the person you are now.

I love what I do!

List everything about your job or favorite pastime that is fulfilling or enjoyable (even if it's only that you appreciate your paycheck).

I love what I do!

Visualize your ideal job or pastime, and describe exactly what you're doing and how you feel about it.

I am grateful for my home
and love living here.

List everything about the place where you live that you enjoy and appreciate.

I am grateful for my home and love living here.

Write a vivid description of your dream home. What makes it special to you, and how does it feel to be living in it?

I let go of all urges to criticize myself.

Your soul mate is sitting in front of you and can hear all your self-critical thoughts. What would that person say to you?

I let go of all urges to criticize myself.

Promise yourself to start noticing and focusing on your best qualities. Begin by making a list right now.

I see each new challenge as an opportunity to become a better me.

Explain what you have learned in life or how you've grown because of problems you've had to solve.

I see each new challenge as an opportunity to become a better me.

Who would you be if you could always see a new problem as a new opportunity?

I forgive myself.

Thinking of mistakes or regrets from your past, how would you forgive others who had done the same?

I forgive myself.

Write a letter of forgiveness to yourself, using all the compassion you would have in forgiving someone else that you love.

I peacefully let go of old memories that no longer serve me.

Write a farewell letter to a disturbing memory, explaining that it no longer has the power to control you in the present.

I peacefully let go of old memories that no longer serve me.

Imagine watching from the beach as your old memories wash out to sea, and describe the peaceful feelings gently rolling in.

I accept my family members just as they are.

Who are your favorite family members and why is it easy to like them?

I accept my family members just as they are.

Which family members are most difficult to accept? Releasing all judgment, list all of the good qualities you can choose to focus on.

I release all resentment toward others.

Write a letter forgiving someone who has wronged you in some way.

I release all resentment toward others.

Take a deep breath, imagine being completely free from the burdens of resentment, and describe how you feel.

I always look for the good in everyone around me.

Think of people you've encountered this past week, including strangers, and write something positive about each one.

I always look for the good in everyone around me.

Describe how it feels to go through a typical day and discover admirable qualities in everyone you meet.

I have wonderful friends, and we all help and support each other.

In what ways do you and your friends show up for each other in good times and bad?

I have wonderful friends, and we all help and support each other.

Imagine your friendships have grown even stronger and more supportive. Explain why you value these relationships more than ever before.

I remain tranquil even in times of turmoil.

If you could travel to the most tranquil destination on earth, where would you go? Describe this place and everything about it that makes you feel peaceful.

I remain tranquil even in times of turmoil.

If you don't already have a happy place you can go to in your mind, create one now. What does it look like, who is there, and how are you feeling?

I have fun and laugh every day.

When was the last time you laughed out loud? Remember that moment and describe your thoughts and emotions.

I have fun and laugh every day.

List 5 crazy things that the kid inside you would love to do for fun.

I sincerely appreciate all the good things in my life.

List 5 things in your life that make you feel grateful.

I sincerely appreciate all the good thing in my life.

Name one thing you've always wanted to be, do, or have. Imagine yourself living that experience now, and write a letter expressing your deep appreciation.

I honor my body as the temple of my soul and treat it with utmost respect.

If your body could write you a letter, what would it thank you for, and what requests might it make?

I honor my body as the temple of my soul and treat it with utmost respect.

Imagine caring for yourself exactly as you would care for a child you love dearly. What would change, and how would you be treated better?

I feel healthy, fit, and strong.

Choose a body part (limb, organ, etc.) and write a letter thanking it for serving you so well.

I feel healthy, fit, and strong.

Imagine yourself in perfect physical shape. What are you able to do that you couldn't do before, and how does that feel?

I have abundant energy.

*What events or circumstances make you feel most energetic?
Why?*

I have abundant energy.

Imagine living through an ordinary day with extraordinary energy. Describe how you feel, from your muscles to your emotions.

I am replacing harmful habits with helpful habits.

What new habits would your mind, body or spirit like for you to cultivate?

I am replacing harmful habits with helpful habits.

Imagine that you have already formed a new helpful habit, and describe or draw the new you.

I am strong, confident, and powerful.

Write about a time when you surprised yourself by your ability to achieve or cope with something difficult.

I am strong, confident, and powerful.

Imagine yourself facing a new, unique challenge with unshakeable confidence. How does it feel to be this new person?

I release limiting beliefs that prevent me from acknowledging my own abilities.

Today is National Brag On Yourself Day. Without reservation, name your strengths and write about what you do best.

I release limiting beliefs that prevent me from acknowledging my own abilities.

Ask close friends and colleagues "What do you think I'm good at?" Make a list, and reread it often.

I choose progress over perfection, and I am at peace.

List some baby steps you've taken toward a goal or desire, and then write a letter congratulating you for making a start.

I choose progress over perfection, and I am at peace.

In recognition of your newfound self-respect, write your declaration of independence from the tyrannical kingdom of perfectionism.

I release my fear of failure and embrace my ability to succeed.

Write a polite farewell to your fear of failure, thank it for trying to protect you, and explain why its services are no longer needed.

I release my fear of failure and embrace my ability to succeed.

Draw yourself accepting an award for your pioneering achievement. Write a gracious acceptance speech.

My fear is only a thought, and I can change my thoughts.

Imagine that your inner child is still afraid of the monster under the bed, and gently explain why there is really nothing to fear.

My fear is only a thought, and I can change my thoughts.

Thinking of your greatest fear now, who would you be without that fear? Describe this new, fearless you.

I am always relaxed and open to going with the flow of life.

Draw yourself floating down a river, aware of the power of the stream yet feeling perfectly safe, calm, and relaxed.

I am always relaxed and open to going with the flow of life.

You peacefully float around a river bend and encounter a completely unexpected surprise. What is the shocking but wonderful new experience that you discover?

I am grateful for all my achievements, even the smallest ones.

List 5 things you've done that made you proud of yourself.

I am grateful for all my achievements, even the smallest ones.

Picture yourself achieving a meaningful goal. Where are you, what are you doing, and how do you feel deep inside?

I release all negative thoughts about money and graciously invite wealth into my life.

Think of negative clichés about "filthy rich" people. Explain why these sayings are meaningless and would never apply to you.

I release all negative thoughts about money and graciously invite wealth into my life.

Imagine your current wealth has doubled or tripled, and describe the person you are now.

I accept the abundance that is flowing into my life.

Choose one aspect of your life, such as emotional well being, love, finances, etc., and define what abundance in that area means to you.

I accept the abundance that is flowing into my life.

Draw yourself crossing a bridge to receive the abundance you just described, and write about the feelings you are experiencing.

I am intelligent, capable, and competent.

Describe your attitude and the emotions you experience when you are doing what you do best.

I am intelligent, capable, and competent.

If you could approach any challenge with those same positive thoughts and feelings, who would you be?

I am learning to be fearless.

Name something you're afraid to try, and list all the reasons you want to step outside of your comfort zone.

I am learning to be fearless.

Envision yourself living in a new, expanded comfort zone and describe all the benefits you are experiencing.

I am free to choose, and today I choose to be happy.

Name something in the past that worried you but never happened. Explain how it feels to be free to choose other thoughts.

I am free to choose, and today I choose to be happy.

Kindly ask your current worries to step aside, and list all the positive, productive thoughts you could choose instead.

I am the captain of my own ship and relish my freedom.

List your lifelong goals, big and small, and mark each one as a "want to" or a "supposed to".

I am the captain of my own ship and relish my freedom.

List the goals that no longer hold meaning for you, and write a permission slip granting you the freedom to let them go without guilt.

I have the courage to live in the truth of who I am.

Who is the person that you've been taught to believe you "should" be.

I have the courage to live in the truth of who I am.

Imagine being free of all conditioned behavior, and describe the person you are now.

I experience joy and create joy for others.

Describe all the various ways that you define joy.

I experience joy and create joy for others.

Picture yourself sharing a joyful moment with others. Describe their reaction, the looks on their faces, and the emotions you are feeling.

I attract only pleasant, positive people into my life.

List the most positive people in your life and why you like them.

I attract only pleasant, positive people into my life.

Imagine having the ideal relationship. What draws you to this person, and how does it feel to spend time together?

I am passionate about living life to the fullest.

Who are people you admire for living adventurous lives? What do they do, and why does it fascinate you?

I am passionate about living life to the fullest.

Choose a big, bold item from your bucket list, and describe yourself living it.

I am the number one fan of me, and all my thoughts are positive and supportive.

Draw yourself as a cheerleader and make up a chant for cheering yourself to victory.

I am the number one fan of me, and all my thoughts are positive and supportive.

In what area of your life could you use a little moral support? Write a positive, encouraging statement, and memorize it.

I am making the world a better place by being a positive influence.

If you could do one thing to make the world a better place, what would it be?

I am making the world a better place by being a positive influence.

List 5 ways you can set a better example of keeping a positive attitude in your day-to-day life.

I celebrate each new day as a rare and precious gift.

If you had only one day to live, what would you do?

I celebrate each new day as a rare and precious gift.

Name 3 ways you can bring more of what you value most into your daily life.

I have the power to create my own life.

What pleases you most about the life you have already created for yourself?

I have the power to create my own life.

What makes you feel good about the new life you are creating for yourself now?

I believe in myself.

What would you do if you were 100% certain that you would succeed?

I believe in myself.

With fearless abandon, describe your wildest, craziest dream and how it feels to be living it.

I am at peace with the universe.

Describe your beliefs about spirituality.

I am at peace with the universe.

List 5 things that make you feel fulfilled in a spiritual sense.

I am happy, joyous and free, exactly as I was meant to be.

Be present in this moment, and describe the happiness, joy, and freedom that are always available to you.

I am happy, joyous and free, exactly as I was meant to be.

Describe a day in your ideal life. Go into detail using all your senses - sight, sound, smell, touch, taste - and explain the emotions you feel.

Notes ...

Notes ...

Spread the word so others can benefit too!

If you enjoyed this journal, please leave a review on Amazon. I'm a freelance writer with no "big marketing company" backing me, so I would greatly appreciate your review, and it will only take you a few minutes.

Here's how to submit a review:
1. Go to Amazon and in the "BOOKS" category, search for:

   Positive Affirmations Journal: 100 Journal Writing Prompts *(be sure the author is Susan LaBorde)*

   Click on this book title to go the detail page.

2. In the Customer Reviews section of the page, click on **Write a customer review**.

3. Then just write your review, and click **Submit**.

Thank you in advance!

Peace,
Susan

---

www.MakeAVisionBoard.com

Visit us on the web to learn about more ways to create a better life for yourself:

- Find out what a vision board is and how to make one.
- Get topic ideas and learn about Gratitude Boards.
- See options for vision board apps and software.
- Explore our "Being, Doing, Having" blog for more about affirmations, happiness, limiting beliefs, mind power, the law of attraction, quality personal growth resources and much more!

http://makeavisionboard.com